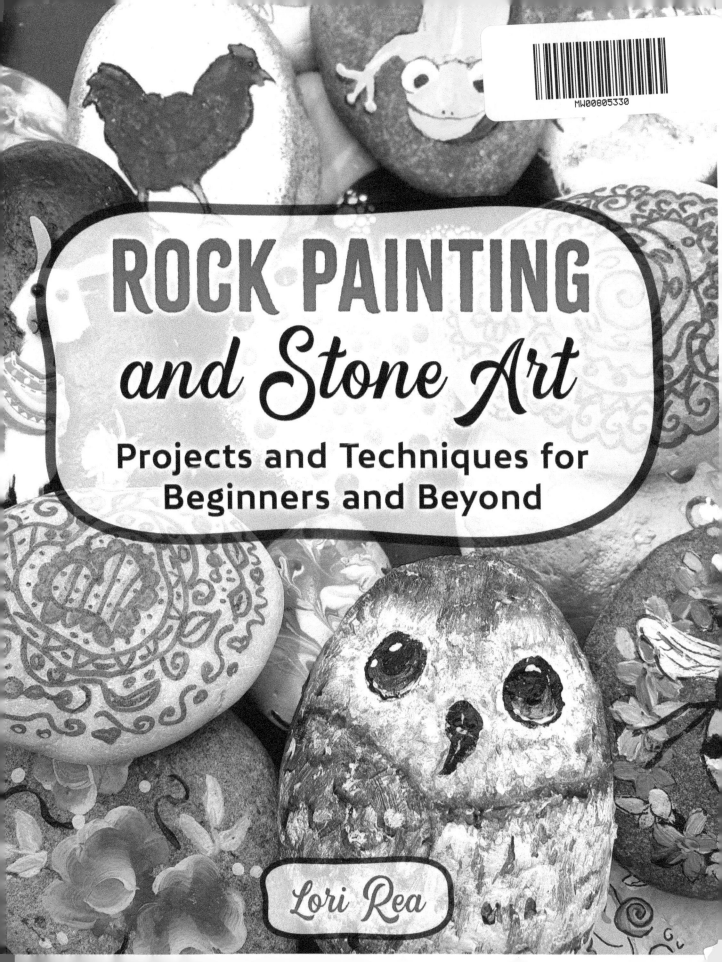

ROCK PAINTING
and Stone Art

Projects and Techniques for Beginners and Beyond

Lori Rea

First published in the United States of
America by Lori Rea

ISBN: 978-1-7343141-2-0

If your stencil has a sticky back, press it onto the rock. If it has no sticky back you can spray it with a spray-on adhesive.

Using a small sponge applicator, pick up some yellow paint with the sponge, lightly press on a sheet of paper to get rid of the excess and then begin to dab/press down the sponge gently onto the stencil. Do not over saturate the sponge with paint as the paint will leak under the stencil and distort the design.

With the paint still slightly wet, pick up some brown paint and fill the middle of the flower. To shade the flower allow the sponge to go into the edge of the petals with the brown. This provides a shading effect.

This stencil has a separate leaf pattern that you can apply. You can see from the picture that it is sometimes difficult to get a stencil to stick to the curve of the rock. You can remedy this by holding down the stencil with one hand and painting with the other.

Discover how EASY and FUN rock painting can be with step-by-step tutorials

Be Inspired....

Over 70 creative ideas ranging from beginner to intermediate.

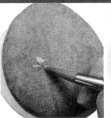

I admit, I am partial to bees. Bees are suffering now and without bees our world is doomed, so get out there and save the bees and while your at it, pick up a rock and celebrate the work they do by painting this.

To make the violets, pick up a dab of dark purple paint and a dab of white paint on the end of a round brush. In just one stroke, you will combine the colors together and make a striated petal.

Contents

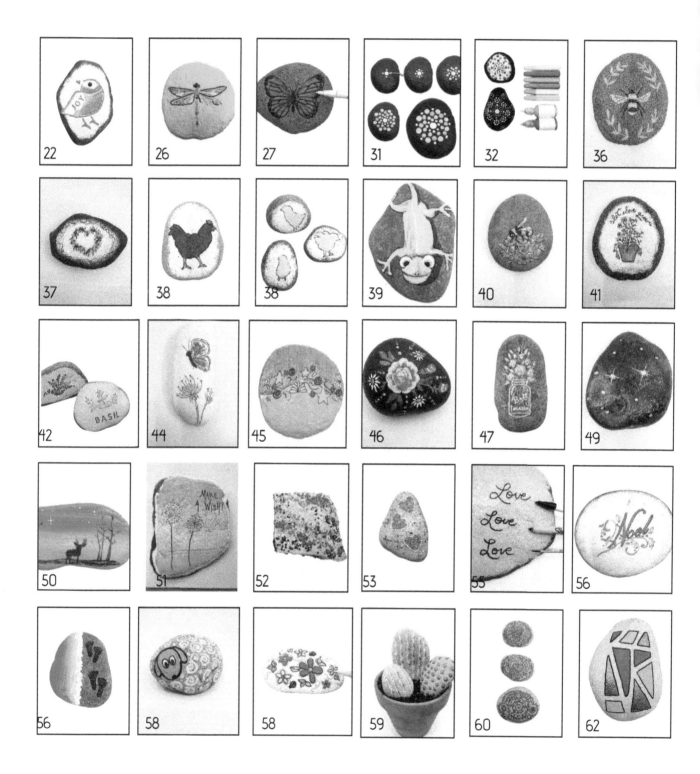

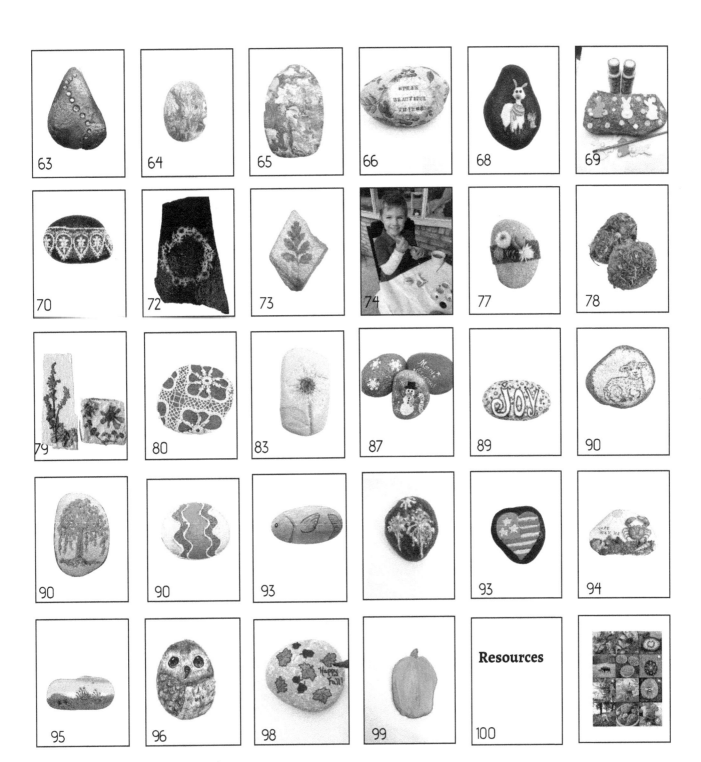

63

64

65

66

68

69

70

72

73

74

77

78

79

80

83

87

89

90

90

90

93

93

94

95

96

98

99

Resources

100

"Creativity is
contagious,
pass it on"

-Albert Einstein

Dedicated to:
Eleanor and Sophia

The mountains near me have towers of rock that soar above the landscape, they are the dominating feature here in the Black Hills.

My frequent hikes bring me much in the way of inspiration for rock painting. Need a fresh perspective or some creative ideas? Get out into whatever nature you have around you, breath deeply and let go of the stress. Ideas will flow.

Eco-Crafting   **Nature Art**   **Green Crafting**

This book is the third published in a series of seven books, all focused on nature crafts and sustainable living. In the last few years there has been a renaissance of making art and crafts with natural materials. My mission, through my books and classes, is to show everyone how fantastic it is to create art with nature. Nature crafts are eco-friendly, sustainable, and inexpensive.

As a child of the 1970's, living in California, I was at the epicenter of the "Back to the land" movement. My fourth-grade teacher was a hippie that loved macrame, maxi skirts and art made with recycled materials. I loved that woman and she taught me a lot.

The 1990's brought us big box craft stores and all kinds of new, manufactured crafting supplies. This was fun, but it left dried flowers and upcycling in the dust.

Fast forward to today and the sustainable, "back to nature" movement has come full circle and now enjoys a new look and a hipster touch. Creating with nature is becoming popular once again.

My goal is to bring the joy of **nature crafts** back into everyday living. Gifts, home décor and objets d'art can all fall comfortably under this banner. It's time to take back crafting from the big box stores and reclaim the treasures of the earth for creative art. So enjoy rock painting! Rocks are some of the most elementary and available natural materials on the planet.

Introduction

Rock art is more than simply painting on rocks, it's a process of gathering, preparing, imagining and creating.

Ambling through the woodland or seashore, bending down to gather up small, earth-created canvases just waiting for your artistic touch, is all a part of the rock art experience.

As you bring your treasures home, and start to envision your designs, your creativity begins to burst forth in new ways. Your mind unplugs from the relentless digital world and relaxes as you center your thoughts on creating something with materials sourced from nature.

Many studies tout the numerous benefits of spending time outdoors and it is my personal belief, after having taught many nature-based art classes, that making art with natural materials can bring a similar reward.

Creating on something as uncomplicated and unpretentious as a rock, helps people to unwind and reconnect with the natural world around them.

Rocks are inexpensive, easily sourced and the pressure to be perfect is absent. It's just a rock, so let go, relax and let the paint flow.

This book is meant to be used as a guide and a source for inspiration. It is a launching pad for your creative journey and hopefully a spark to help you develop your own passion for rock painting.

I wanted to write a book that was more than just painting on rocks, so this is a rock painting and stone art book. It is completely unique among rock art books in that it not only gives you comprehensive instructions on rock painting but it takes you BEYOND and into the world of creating rock art with clay, pressed flowers, fiber art and more.

I define **rock painting** under a broad banner, with the use of all types of art mediums: acrylic paint, oil pens and markers.

Stone art is the term used when a rock is decorated in some way other than painting. For example: decoupage, crochet, pressed flowers and stickers.

Rock Story

I was seven years old when I first started painting on rocks. My grandmother, a wise woman, knew I was eager to paint so she introduced me to the inexpensive and readily available, humble rock canvas.

That summer I sat in her art studio and painted my heart out. I recruited other neighborhood children to canvas the suburbs of New Jersey to find more rocks to paint and I "paid" them by giving them access to my grandmothers studio to create with us.

As an adult, I've taught my own children and many others how to paint with rocks. I never get tired of seeing those happy, free faces as they make something that brings them joy.

I think many of those that call themselves artists, or at least lay claim to an artistic hobby, can often connect it to a time in their childhood when they felt the joy and freedom of creating without expectation or pressure, when enthusiasm was the pure motivation.

The Basics:
Rocks,
Paint, Tools

Finding Rocks

It seems so simple when you first think about painting rocks; you just go outside and pick a few up, right?

However, there are many people that don't live in an area with an abundance of paintable stones. Getting your rocks free and from nature is the best way to source rocks, but if you can't do that there are other options.

Nature

This is the obvious and best way to get rocks. Get outside and look around. If you have kids you can make looking for rocks like a treasure hunt.

Please be careful where you pick up rocks. Many natural areas and parks have rules about not removing any natural resources. Also be careful not to pick up rocks out of private landscaping areas or areas that might be sprayed with weed killing chemicals.

Landscape Companies and Garden Centers

These are great sources of rocks that will usually allow you to pick your own and weigh them out for purchase. It's usually the most inexpensive option (other than finding your own).

Craft Stores

Some craft stores carry rocks for painting but they tend to be on the smaller side.

Online

Buying rocks online is easier and more economical than you think! Check on Google, Amazon and Etsy for sellers that sell "river rocks for painting".

Finding, Choosing and Preparing Rocks

Choosing rocks
can be as simple as picking up a rock that inspires you to be creative. Any shape will do but most people like rocks that are smooth. River rocks, as they are sometimes called, are the coveted smooth, circular rocks that everyone wants but I find it fun to be creative with rocks that have irregular shapes as well.

Throughout this book I have purposely chosen rocks for projects that are not perfectly round because that just doesn't always happen in real life.

Use what's available in your area and remember that the rocks that don't have a perfect circumference need love too. Sometimes the misshapen ones actually inspire more creativity.

Preparing Rocks for Painting
Rocks can be washed with water or a simple dishsoap solution. Bleach is rarely necessary unless you are concerned about bacteria. Use a scrub brush to remove dirt, if needed.

Wash your rocks outside if you can, it's great to use the garden hose and apply pressure to get out the debris and dirt. Let the rocks dry fully before painting.

USE WHAT YOU HAVE! IT'S ALL GOOD!

Permanent markers,
regular and fine tip,
good for outlining

Paints and Pens and Tools

Rock painting requires only some paint and a brush, but as any crafter knows, the materials and tools list can expand rapidly! I am a minimalist so I tend to like to keep things simple but neither do I judge those who love stocking up on the fun extras! After you read this chapter, go online and look up "rock painting tools" and you will be amazed what the humble rock has inspired from legions of crafts companies.

Paints

The favorite paint for painting on rocks is acrylic paint. These paints usually come in bottles or tubes and they are sold in different thicknesses. "Craft" paints are thinner and flow more easily and "tube acrylics" are thicker and provide better coverage. I use both types and keep them on hand.

Paint Pens

Paint pens come in two types: oil and water based.
Oil pens go on more thickly, are permanent and can be used on bare rock.
Water based pens tend to not be as thick and sometimes need to have several applications to show up well (on bare rock). They usually must have a base coat on the rock to be seen as the natural rock base absorbs this paint readily.

Markers

Markers come in an astounding array of colors and can be used on bare, unpainted rock as well as those with a base coat. They are great for outlining and making zentangle designs. Be careful when you put sealant on them, sealants tend to make markers run.

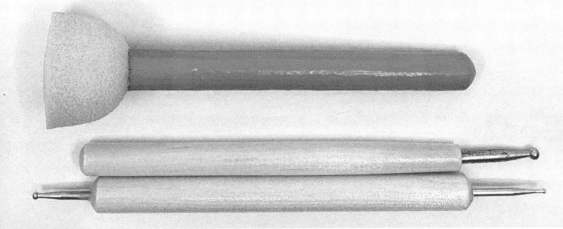

Brushes

If you are just starting out in painting, I recommend buying a medium quality, combination set of brushes that have a variety of types in it such as: rounds, flats, filberts and shaders. Buy a set whose brush sizes are on the smaller side as rocks are generally not too large.

Dauber sponges are short sticks with small sponges on the end that create circles of varying sizes.

Sponges come is a multitude of shapes and sizes. I like to always keep a variety of stenciling sponges on hand.

Dotting tools come in a variety of sizes. They are sometimes called stylus pens. You don't need special tools though, you can use pencils, nails and Q-tips as well.

Stamps

I couldn't do without letter stamps, I use them in so many projects. They are inexpensive and I buy them in a variety of font styles. Stamps with objects on them (flowers, animals, etc...) are fun to use on rocks. Smaller stamps work better than larger sizes as large stamps don't always cover the rock surface well.

Stickers

Some brands stick better than others but generally all stickers will need a clear top coat or extra glue on the back. Stickers work best with an undercoat of paint on the rock. 3-dimensional stickers are fun to use as well but they will not lay flat or take sealant and cannot be used outdoors.

Stencils

These are readily available in craft stores and online. I like the type that have sticky backs as this is generally needed for a rock's uneven surface.

Decoupage

You can use napkins, thin paper and fabric for decoupage. I collect various paper ephemera and keep pieces that are good for decoupage.

Hairdryer

A very handy tool to have for impatient painters as it speeds up drying time significantly.

Base coat

There are two ways to base coat a rock with paint: Spray painting or brush on painting. For whichever method you choose, make sure the rock is clean of debris and dry before you start.

To **spray paint**: hold the spray can approximately 12" away from the rock. Spray a white or black spray paint/primer onto the rock lightly. After the first coat is dry you can do a second or third coat. Spraying too heavily will make the paint run and drip.

This is an efficient method as you can do many rocks at once and this leaves a smooth, even finish. Spray outside in a well ventilated area.

To **Brush on** the base coat, make sure the rock is clean and dry before painting.
Using acrylic paint, apply a first coat.
After the first coat is dry, and if a second coat is needed, apply a second coat.
You can seal the base coat if you wish with spray or brush on sealant.

If you wish to keep the **natural color** of the rock you are painting on, you can still seal it first. Sealing it helps the paint design to go on more smoothly and you can also wipe off any mistakes. If you paint a naked rock (I think naked rocks do have a great, earthy tone) and you make a mistake, it can't be wiped off.
Use a clear, spray on sealant and spray it on lightly.

Sealants and Varnishes

The paint on rocks tends to fade over time, especially if the rock is going to be displayed outdoors. Sealants help to preserve your paintings and protect them from fading and chipping.

There are different kinds of sealants and some work better than others for different types of mediums. For example, almost all sealants work with acrylic paint but not all sealants work with markers. Some sealants make markers "bleed" or "run" (see photo on right). You need to TEST the sealants before you spray them on your designs. I don't recommend specific brands for the broad term of "markers" because markers come in so many different ink types. I have used sealants that said they were safe for ink, and they weren't. So do a test on a small rock before you spray your entire piece.

Make sure your piece is completely dry before you attempt any sealants or varnishes. If you don't wait until your piece is dry, it could make the elements (paint, pens, etc...) run together and muddle.

There are several things to consider when choosing a sealant.

Spray on sealants are easy to use but they do create fumes and should be used outside. Spray about 12" away from the project and do several, light coats or it will tend to make drip marks.

Popular brands include Rust-oleum-Triple Thick Glaze ™ (glossy) and Design Master Clear Finish™ (Matte).

Brush on is a liquid that can be applied with a paintbrush. It's generally not as smelly and it can go on in one coat (most of the time). Popular brands include Mod Podge ™ and Americana DuraClear ™.

Both sprays and brush on come in two types:

Gloss will give you a shiny, bright surface that reflects light.

Matt is a softer, non-glossy look that is subtle with no sheen.

Sealants can be purchased at hardware and craft stores. I suggest getting at least two types to have on hand.

Ruined because I didn't test the sealant!

Test how a sealant will react to your art medium by making a doodle with the medium on another rock or paper, waiting till it's dry and then spraying with your sealant. If it runs, don't use it!

Projects

Tools and Techniques

Tools for stenciling are extremely simple: A stencil template, a sponge applicator and paint.

If your stencils do not come with adhesive backing, you can use a **spray-on adhesive** if you wish. Rocks are usually uneven surfaces so adhesive of some kind is needed.

Stencils are sold in all major craft stores or they can be purchased online.

Acrylic craft paint works best for stenciling.

A **sponge applicator** is an inexpensive item that has a small sponge on a stick. You can use a household sponge but it is difficult to cut it small enough for rock painting.

Stenciling Tips

The stencils I've chosen to use in this book are designs that are readily available, albeit with slight differences, from several companies.

When stenciling, one important thing to remember is that too much paint on the sponge translates to paint bleed underneath the stencil and a blurring of the design. So, use paint sparingly. Dip the sponge applicator lightly into the paint, dab the sponge onto the paper towel and then apply to the stencil.

It's best to practice stenciling on paper first before you work on the uneven surface of a rock.

You can leave the rock natural or base coat it first with paint. The only con to using a natural, uncoated rock is that if you make a mistake with the paint, you can't wipe it off.

Smoothness matters when it comes to stenciling on rocks! Uneven surfaces are difficult to stencil on.

Simple Stencil

Start with a smooth, clean rock. Your rock can be natural, natural with a sealant applied or base coated with acrylic.

If your stencil has a sticky back, press it onto the rock. If it has no sticky back you can spray it with a spray-on adhesive. You can also apply tape to the edges of the stencil if you wish but sometimes the tape does not stick.

Using a small sponge applicator, pick up some yellow paint, lightly press on a sheet of paper to get rid of the excess paint and then begin dabbing/ pressing down the sponge gently onto the stencil. Do not over saturate the sponge with paint as the paint will leak under the stencil and distort the design.

With the paint still slightly wet, pick up some brown paint with the sponge and dab it in the middle of the flower. To shade the flower, allow the sponge to go into the edge of the petals with the brown. This gives a shaded effect.

This stencil has a separate leaf pattern that you can apply. You can see from the picture that it is sometimes difficult to get a stencil to stick to the curve of the rock. You can remedy this by holding down the stencil with one hand and painting with the other.

Wash your stencils after use by wiping them down with a wet paper towel. The paint usually comes off well if it hasn't been dried on the stencil for too long.

Same Stencil - 2 Ways

To stencil this bird, use the same basic instructions as for the flower on the opposite page.

This bluebird project shows how the stencil looks in two different styles.

The natural, minimalist bird with no base coat and no outlining is a softer look.

The bird on the white background with blue outlining stands out more.

Tip:
When creating with stencils and paint, think about incorporating markers into the mix by using them for outlining, adding color, etc...

Dragonfly Stencil

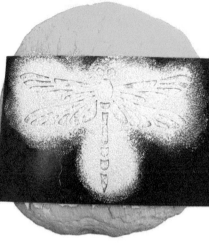

This stencil uses both a sponge and a small paintbrush.

Begin by base-coating the rock a light green.

Apply the stencil and go over the entire area with a sponge, dipped in white.

For more delicate/small areas of the stencil, use a small stencil brush or a small paint brush. Using the brush, pick up the color desired and dab the brush on a paper towel to rid of the excess. Apply the colors.

Work carefully so that the paint does not bleed under the design.

After the design is dry, use a fine point sharpie marker to outline the details. I sometimes add more detail than is found in the stencil by adding legs, antennae, etc...

Add thin, white lines between the colors with a liner brush.

This type of stencil technique turns out to look more like a painting than a simple stencil.

When using mixed mediums (paint + markers) make sure the sealant you use won't make the marker bleed.

Stenciled, Shaded Butterfly

This butterfly is an example of how to shade a stencil by adding layers of color.

Start by firmly pressing the stencil to the natural or base-coated rock.

The first application of paint, using a sponge, is an acrylic, bright orange. While the orange paint is still wet, use a small amount of yellow and lightly sponge around the outer edge of the wings.

While the wings are still wet, use a clean sponge and pick up black paint and go around the outer edges of the wings and the middle of the body.

After the stencil dries, take a black paint pen and outline the inner and outer areas of the wings.

Using a white paint pen, make small white dots around the edge of the wings.

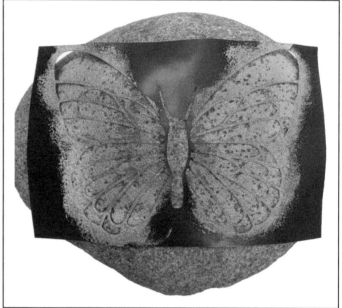

The paint pens used in this project are oil based.

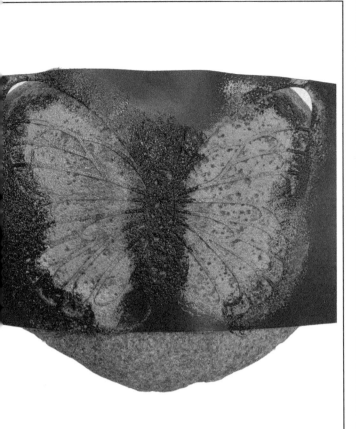

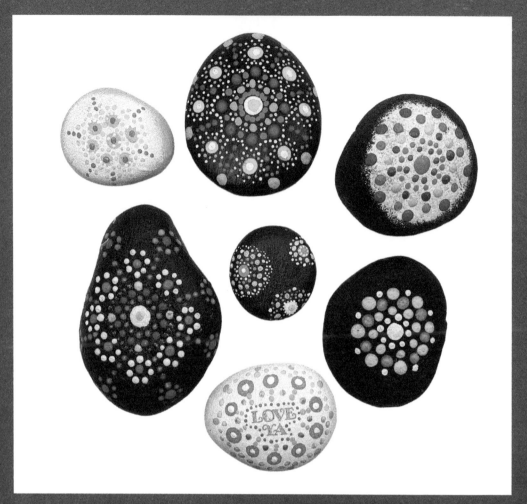

Dot painting and Mandalas

Dot painting is enjoyable and almost zen like, and at first glance it looks very simple to do. However, getting the paint to the correct thickness and choosing the right tool can be challenging at first.

It's helpful to practice a little with a piece of paper before you work on your rock.

The best paint to use for dot painting is acrylic craft paint. The craft paint (as opposed to the tube acrylic) tends to be a bit thinner and it goes on more evenly.

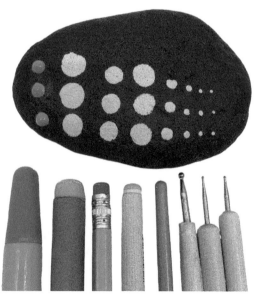

There are special tools for mandala painting called dotting styluses. You can buy these tools in almost any size and they are very handy. However, you can also use things like: pencil erasers, the ends of paint brushes, paint pens, daubing tools, nails and even Nerf darts! The picture on the left gives you an idea of dot sizes from various tools.

Simple Mandala

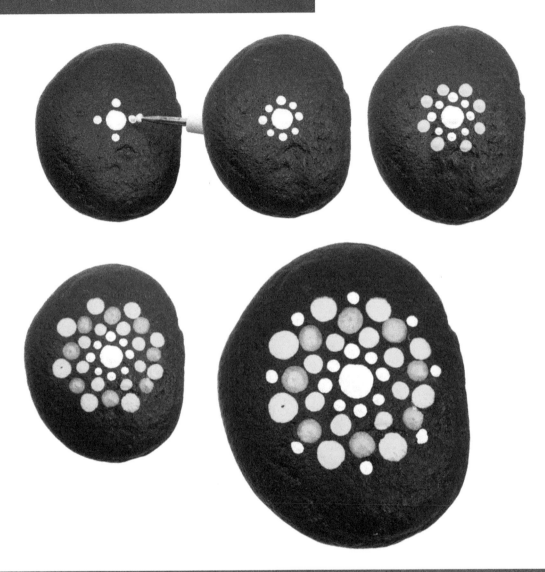

Mandalas can be very difficult to get completely perfect and I'm not a perfectionist so I usually mess up a little on each one I make. But most mandalas look great, even if they aren't 100% perfect. My friends that are perfectionists absolutely love mandala painting.

If you've never tried a mandala before, you'll want to start with a very simple design for the best chance of success.

To make a mandala, begin with a center dot.

Start the next color/dot layer next to the center dot and complete a circle around the center dot.

With each new color added, you will be going in a complete circle around the center.

Always finish the circle with one color and layer before starting another one.

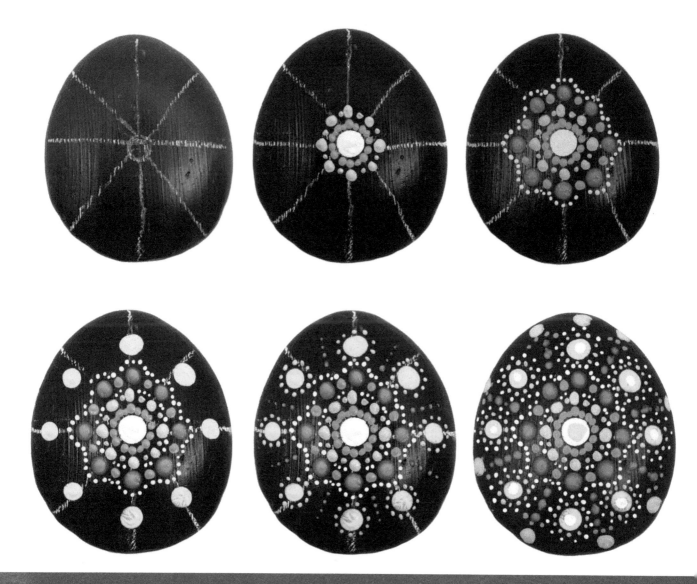

Mandala with Line Guides

To Paint a more complicated mandala, using a piece of chalk, draw a circle in the center and then draw lines at even spaces around the center. It is helpful to use a ruler if your stone is large enough and even enough.

Line up your first few layers of dots with the chalk lines to keep things evenly spaced.

Keep adding dots in different sizes and colors. Always finish the circumference of a circle before starting the next color.

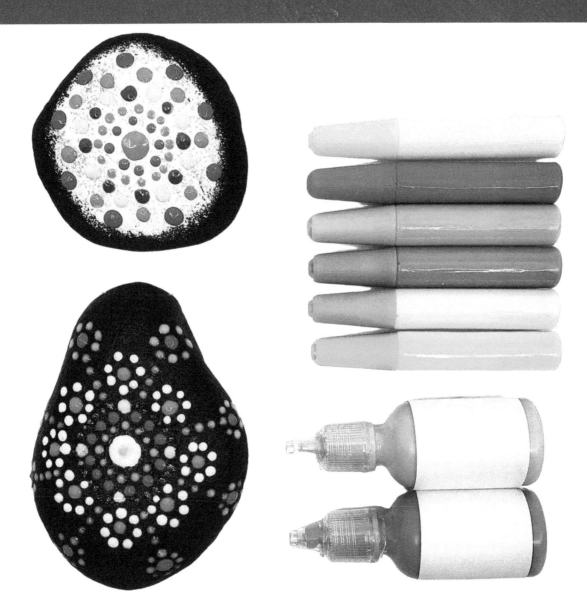

Puffy paints

Puffy paints give a raised texture to dot painting. Acrylic paint is flat, puffy paints are thick. This gives a very different look and feel to your dot painting. Personally, I think using puffy paint for dot painting is actually easier in some ways. However, the size of a dot can be a bit difficult to control but this is easily remedied with a special writing tip you can purchase specifically for puffy paints.

Practice with puffy paints and get the feel for controlling the flow of paint before you start on your project.

Freehand Painting

Freehand painting is the most common type of painting on rocks. For the most part it's just you, the brush, some paint and your imagination.

Technically freehand painting means: drawn or executed by hand without guiding instruments, measurements, or other aids.

This type of painting gives the most room for artistic expression and ideas.

Freehand painting lets your imagination soar but if your imagination isn't soaring you can always use Pinterest or internet images to help get it going.

Make sure you have an assortment of at least 4 types of brushes on hand: round, flat, liner/rigger and filbert. Generally you will want to stick with smaller size brushes as rocks are generally more diminutive.

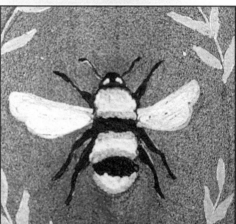 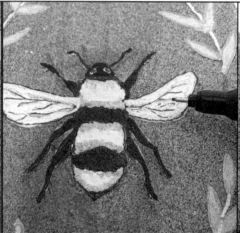 

Queen Bee

Part of the appeal of this bee painting is the natural gray background of the rock. I "test" my designs on Instagram and this got a big, positive response.

To make this bee I used both acrylic paint and paint pens.

When you want to get proportions on your designs just right, do an online search for a silhouette of the thing you want to paint, in this case a bee. Print out the silhouette and cut it out, place it on the rock and do a light pencil tracing around the outside of the cut out. After the pencil tracing, go around the pencil with a white paint pen.

Paint the leaves a light green. The bee is yellow, black and white.

To shade the bee, use a light tan on the edges of the black. The wings have very light yellow lines that you can do with a liner/rigger brush.

Using a black, fine tip permanent marker, go around the bee and outline it. Use the pen to draw very fine webbing on the wing.

Outline the leaves with a gold paint pen (black would work as well).

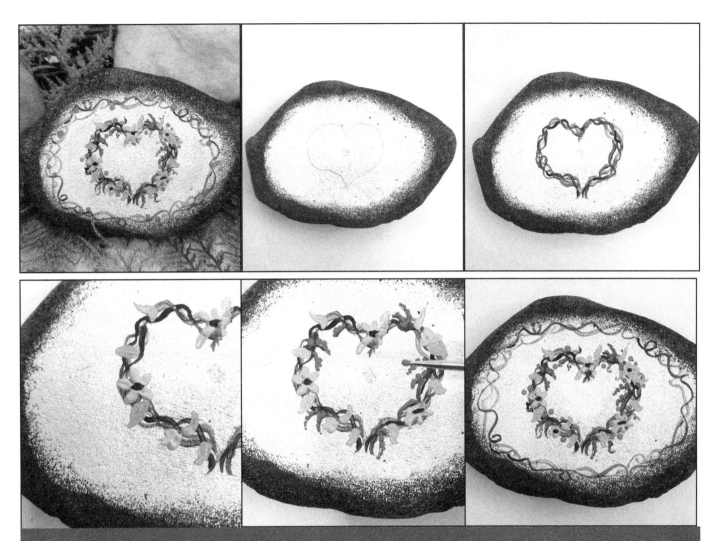

It's always enjoyable to paint wreaths. Wreaths are where you can let your creativity run wild.

For this wreath-rock, sponge coat a light base of white. Lightly outline a heart or circle with pencil.

Using a fine liner/rigger brush, begin to paint thin lines around the penciled heart in two different colors of brown.

After the wreath is dry, begin to add flowers and leaves.

5-petal flowers can be very simple, short brush strokes. Press your brush at the center of the flower then slightly lift up the brush, as the stroke ends. Do that five times around in a circle. Other flowers are great just as small dots in various patterns and colors.

You can paint a grapevine frame around the outer edge if desired.

Grapevine
Wreath

Sponge a light white background on the rock and then trace the silhouette of a chicken with a permanent black marker.

This hen is a Rhode Island Red. Paint the body of the hen with a dark, brownish red. The legs are yellow, the beak is orange, and the comb is bright red.

Hen

Chicks

It's super cute to give the hen some little chicks. Pick out 3 similar colored rocks that are a few sizes smaller and go through the same steps except make the bodies light yellow.

Paint the legs and beaks orange.
Add detail to the chicks with a very fine black marker.

Lizard Rock

This big-eyed lizard is fun to put in the garden and watch visitors do a second glance.

This lizard looks most realistic if it's on an unpainted background.

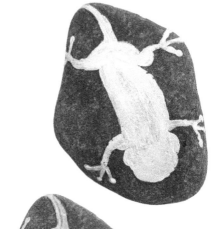

Use a paper silhouette to trace or sketch the lizard in pencil then fill in with white paint.

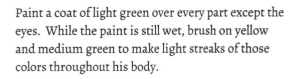

Paint a coat of light green over every part except the eyes. While the paint is still wet, brush on yellow and medium green to make light streaks of those colors throughout his body.

The eyes are a light orange/tan.

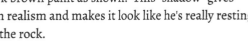

Outline the body in a thin, dark brown, fine point permanent marker. Add details to the eyes, mouth and nose.

Add a shadow to the right side of the lizard with a dark brown paint as shown. This "shadow" gives him realism and makes it look like he's really resting on the rock.

I admit, I am partial to bees. Bees are suffering now and without bees our world is doomed, so get out there and save the bees and while your at it, pick up a rock and celebrate the work they do by painting this.

To make the violets, pick up a dab of dark purple paint and a dab of white paint on the end of a round brush. In just one stroke, you will combine the colors together and make a striated petal. Starting at the middle of the circle of a flower, press lightly down on your brush and pull downwards. The colors will mix together. Lift your brush up gently as you finish the stroke.

For the leaves, use some light green and paint in and around the violets. Make sure the violets are dry before you start.

Add small yellow circles to the middle of each flower.

Using black paint, begin making the body of the bee as shown.

Next, add the yellow stripes between the black. Don't make hard edges, you want the appearance of softness.

Paint the wings with white and add the whites of the eyes.

After it is completely dry, add details with a fine permanent maker: the lacy wing veins, antennae, legs and details of the eyes.

Outline some of the flowers and leaves with the marker as well.

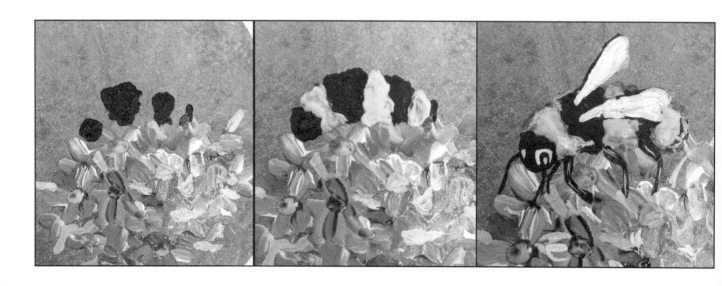

Sponge a white base coat on a flat rock. If you like the color of the rock, don't cover it completely.

Lightly sketch a flower pot with pencil. Fill in the pot with a light rust color. Shade the pot by applying a darker rust color as shown.

Lightly pencil in the stems and flowers.

Paint the stems and leaves a light, medium green.

Add the flowers in a medium or mustard yellow. Add dark brown centers.

After the piece is completely dry, using a fine tip marker, outline the pot, stems and flowers.

The letters are in a free hand cursive, if you don't feel confident in your cursive, use letter stamps or a stamp with wording that you like.

Tip:

Outlining your designs is a great way to not only make your piece stand out, but give the small details more sharpness.

Garden Markers

Garden markers are one of the most practical uses for painted rocks. I love tucking these markers next to plants for guests who wander through the garden and also for confused husbands that have been sent out to pick some herbs for dinner.

You absolutely must use a sealant on these rocks as they will be sitting in the sun the majority of their lives.

Test the sealant to make sure it is compatible with any markers or inks you've used.

There are an infinite variety of ways to make garden markers. Do an internet search of the plants that you want to paint.

For a base coat, I like to keep as much of the natural rock showing as possible, but you can paint the entire rock as well, it's all up to personal preference.

To start, lightly sponge a base coat on the face of the rock.

Look at the plant you wish to paint, either by online photos or the plant itself. Look at the stem and observe the leaf structure. If it's a vegetable, look at its overall shape and color.

Round brushes and liner brushes work well for painting leaves and stems.

After you have painted your plant, stamp the name of it onto the rock or write with a permanent marker.

Go over the plant design with a fine tip permanent marker to outline.

For this set of markers I used oil based paint pens. Oil markers give the letters a rich, deep color.

Watercolor Look with Acrylics

The watercolor look is achieved by using thinned-out acrylic paint that is applied sparingly. You don't need actual watercolor paints to get this look.

Using a permanent fine tip marker, sketch your design onto a rock that has a base coat of white.

Choose your colors and thin the paint. I usually do 2 drops of paint to 1 drop of water ratio. Experiment with your paint to determine the best amount of water for the type of paint you are using.

Lightly drop in the paint with gentle touches, as opposed to the normally used brushstrokes.

Drop small drips of paint into the sketched out areas. Let dry and spray lightly with a sealant that is safe for use with markers.

Get inspired for designs by doing an internet search with the word "images" after it. For example: type in, "butterfly painting images". You can do this on Google or Pinterest.

This rock uses several types of techniques: watercolor, free hand and outlining.

To start, undercoat the rock in a light tan/peach color.

After that is fully dry, thin out some orange paint to a watery consistency. Apply to the top half of the rock.

When dry, add a leaf vine in green.

Begin adding blue star fish, yellow shells, brown curly cues and tiny orange flowers with white accents.

When completely dry you can add another layer of deeper orange to the top.

Outline the objects with a thin, black marker.

Spray on a light coat of sealant.

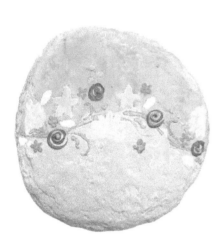

You can make any rock that isn't too heavy into a hanging rock or Christmas ornament.
Carefully glue a piece of: ribbon, thin lace or string to the back.

Simple Stroke Flowers

Painting one-stroke roses is much easier than it looks. It's all about how you load the brush with paint and how you hold and turn the brush as you apply it. Flat or angled brushes are best for this technique. The size of the brush you use will depend on how large you want to make your flower. For this rose tutorial I have used an angle brush in 5/8".

Spray or paint your rock in your chosen background color.

First, put dabs of purple and white acrylic side by side. Dip one half of the brush in dark purple and the other side in light purple. The paint will mix and flow together to create a shaded look when it is applied to the rock.

(1) Press the brush onto the rock and draw it forward, angle the brush down towards your wrist and then push it back up again to create a scalloped look. (2) Build two layers, or circles of petals

(3) To make the bud in the center you will make a stroke that looks a little like a rainbow.

(4) The next stroke starts at the exact edge on the left and pulls down and around towards the right edge and meets up with it. (5) This finishes the rose.

(6) The daisies are simple, one stroke flowers. Press the brush down lightly and draw it upwards as you pull it towards you. This gives the petal a tapered look. Add yellow centers.

(7) The leaves are made in a similar fashion to the daisy petals with a medium green. (8) Add purple dots.

First, draw a mason jar with a white paint pen.

Second, make the roses by drawing small semi circles with a pink pen.

After the pink dries, fill in between the empty areas with the white pen.

Third, draw in the green leaves with a light green pen.

After the leaves dry, add the stems that go into the jar.

Add the red hearts.

Fourth, using a fine line permanent marker, outline the flowers, leaves and hearts.

Paint Pen Flowers

Selling Rocks

Do you want to make money selling your creative designs? You definitely can if you have a little bit of marketing savvy.

Many rocks sellers have success through painting special requests and commissions. Commissions come from people who want things like memorial rocks or pet portraits. Facebook pages, Instagram and Etsy will help people find you online for commissions.

Becoming well known on social media translates into sales because being an influencer in your artistic niche will drive traffic to your Etsy store or website.

Selling and Social Media Platforms

Etsy

Etsy is probably the number one platform most people think about when they are thinking of selling a handmade item.
To sell rocks on Etsy, you need to stand out in some way. You will want to develop a style or niche. Making a name for yourself by specializing in a certain style will help you find customers. Get good at mandalas, or specialize in pet portraits, for example.

It takes a while to get traction on Etsy and you must advertise your Etsy store by way of social media.

Websites

You can set up your own website and sell from it, but generally you will need a way to drive traffic to your site by way of social media. Building and maintaining your own website has never been easier but some sellers don't want to go that route so they use platforms like Etsy, Ebay or Facebook.

Social Media

Facebook, Pinterest, Instagram, Youtube: which social media platform will work best and sell the most for you? I once heard a very wise, rich internet marketer tell his audience, "Find out which social media platform your customers are using and put your energy into that platform."

My personal opinion is that most artists hang out on **Instagram**, which is primarily a visual platform. My next choice would be **Facebook**. **Pinterest** is also a visual media but it is currently more difficult to build an audience there. **Youtube** is great for building a following if you want to make tutorials for people on how to paint rocks.

Craft Shows

Many people prefer to do local, in person selling. Craft shows and galleries are a way to have more contact with your customers. There are pros and cons to hauling merchandise around in your vehicle, setting it all up and taking it down again. I've had fabulous success with some shows and others have been a total bust. Do your research and talk to other craft vendors before you sign up for a show.

Galaxy rocks

The base of the rock is black, spray painted or brushed on. High gloss paint looks best.

Sponge on a light layer of each color. Start the layers with a deep purple, followed by blue, teal and pink/red.

When all those colors have been applied, sponge a streak of black down the middle.

Add the stars with white paint and a fine brush.

Spray with a high gloss sealant to finish.

Just like there are millions of galaxies in the universe, there are also millions of ways to paint a galaxy on a rock! Be creative with colors, stars and planets!

An alternative method for making stars is to use an old toothbrush. Dip the toothbrush in thinned paint and hold over the rock. Run your thumb across the bristles. This will spray the paint onto the rock in a splatter pattern.

Ombre Backgrounds

Ombre backgrounds are a beautiful way to add a base coat to a rock. All types of designs can be added to the top of ombre but my favorite is to add black silhouette paintings.

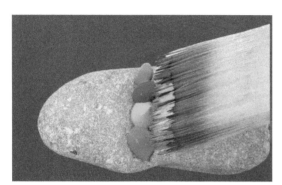 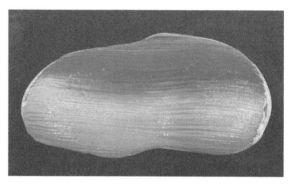

To make an ombre background, choose 2 or 3 coordinating colors in thick, tube acrylics.

Using a wide brush, pull the paint across the rock. You can do this several times to get good coverage and blending.

When dry, spray with a sealant.

Using a thin, liner brush or black marker, draw your outline and then fill in with marker or black paint.

Since you've sealed your rock before adding your design, you should be able to quickly wipe off any mistakes.

After the design has dried, respray with sealant.

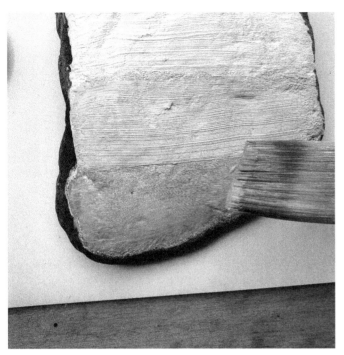

This background is similar to ombre but slightly different. The colors on this rock softly transition from one to another.

Start by sponging on a white base coat. Add your chosen colors one by one (pictured is orange, yellow, light green and medium blue), cleaning the brush after each. Let the colors blend slightly by painting on the next color before the preceding color is dry to create a soft transition.

Paint two white circles, let dry then add dandelion details with a permanent black marker.

The "Make a Wish!" is drawn on with black marker.

Spray with a sealant that is safe for markers.

Note: I put this out in the garden and the kids loved it, however I forgot to spray it with sealant and within a month of sitting in the sun the rock was completely faded. Sealant is important!

Wish Garden Rock

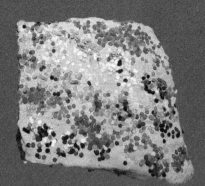

Glitter Rocks

Glitter is messy, fun and it drives a lot of people crazy but I've loved it ever since I was a little kid. Glitter was the most exciting thing about 1st grade art and I'm still making messes with it today.

Applying glitter to rocks can be done in a number of ways, some less messy than others.

My first choice is to spray a rock with spray adhesive, shake the glitter on in the desired area and then spray with adhesive again (lightly).

Kids Tip:

Glitter comes in glue form which is a great thing for kids! It keeps the level of glitter dust down but kids can still have an exciting, glittery experience without the mess.

Another glitter application method is to simply base coat the rock with paint and while the paint is still wet, shake the glitter on it. After the rock is dry, spray it with sealant.

If you really want to go wild, you can buy glitter spray in the form of spray paint, sometimes called "glitter dust".

For the Happy Birthday rock below, the glitter was applied by the spray adhesive method after a coat of base paint.

The "Happy Birthday" banner is a piece of thin, tissue paper to which sticker letters have been applied.

Place the banner on the rock and lightly spray with glue adhesive.

What a great gift for a friend to find on her doorstep the morning of her birthday!

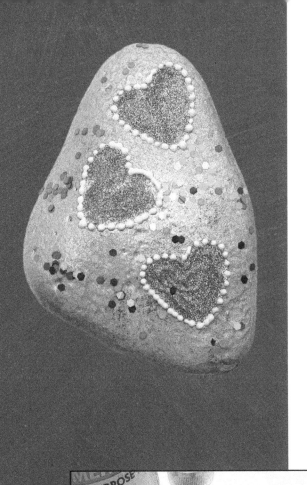

To make this glittery heart rock, start by painting a base coat with a shiny spray paint like this pearl green. Let dry.

Trace 3 hearts in pencil.

Paint the inside of the hearts white.
While the hearts are still wet, shake on fine, gold glitter.

After the gold hearts are dry, shake off the excess glitter and then spray a light coat of adhesive over the rock.

Using a larger size glitter, shake lightly onto the rock, avoiding the hearts.

Puffy paint is used to make tiny dots around the outside of the hearts.

When the dots are fully dry, spray on a protective sealant to protect your design and keep all the glitter in place.

Stamps

Learning to stamp on rocks isn't difficult but there are tips and tricks you need to know to help your projects turn out well.

Tips:

Make sure your stones are very smooth. If the stone is uneven or jagged, stamping won't work well. Stamps require a smooth surface to print well.

Second, make sure to load up plenty of ink onto the stamp, it takes more ink to stamp on rocks than it does on paper.

Third, smaller stamps generally turn out better than larger designs.

Letter stamps to make words are fun to use but don't expect a perfectly even line of text when you are stamping, the curve of the rock makes that very difficult. Go with a more informal look for your letters.

Letter stamps are generally available at big box stores and online at a low cost.

Mix up stamping with other types of painting and media.

Type in "short quotes" into your search engine for great ideas for quotes to use.

Be careful what sealant you use with your inks. Test your sealant first to make sure the ink doesn't run.

Hand Lettering

Paint Pen

Sharpie Marker

Paint brush, acrylic paint

Hand lettering on rocks is beautiful and everyone admires well written sayings.

Writing on rocks can be challenging. The uneven surface of the rock combined with the difficulties of the paint flow often make letters appear choppy.

A great way to practice hand lettering is to buy some practice/tracing sheets on Etsy, or just download a style you like, print it out and practice over it.

The above examples are used to show how each type of writing instrument looks unique.

The Paint pen is fairly easy to write with although I found that sometimes the paint flows out in an erratic way, making the letters fat in one area and thin in others.

Paint pens come in water and oil based pens. The water based pens are more opaque but work well if you have a smooth base coat. Oil based pens are glossy and give great coverage. Always test out your sealants to make sure they won't make the oil based paint run.

The Permanent marker is by far the easiest to control when writing and gives the most even flow to the letters. Marker writing can be more prone to fading when left out in the sun.

Paint is the hardest to control when trying to write with a paintbrush, no matter how thin and fine. It takes a lot of practice to keep the letters consistent looking.

Hand lettering ideas:

Try looking up different fonts and styles online.

Practice your letters with your chosen instrument before you write on your rocks. You can lightly pencil in your letters first before applying a more permanent option.

Spraying a sealant onto the rock **before** you write will give you the ability to wipe off mistakes before they dry.

And finally, enjoy the process and don't expect perfection, you'll be disappointed.

Stamps

Sometimes stamps just don't show up well on a rock, especially if the surface is uneven. You can remedy this by using a matching marker to fill in any uneven areas.

Outline and fill in areas with markers to finish the design.

This rock has been kept natural on one side to suggest a sandy beach. For the ocean side, refer to the ombre painting page and use blue and white. After the ombre is dry, use white paint and go along the edges to make sea foam.

I used a foot stamp but you could also paint the feet as well. I had to fill in a few uneven stamp marks with a black marker.

Tips for working with paint pens

Paint pens are an exciting to use and they can give you more control in the application of paint. Hand lettering, fine details and great coverage are some of the advantages of paint pens.

If you undercoat/paint your rocks first, the paint pens will glide on smoothly. If you don't base coat you will use an oil pen as oils are stronger and brighter when used on an uncoated surface.

Paint pens sometimes have to be "started" by vigorous shaking and also by gently pressing the tip downward to start the flow of paint. Always test the paint pen on a piece of paper first to check the flow rate of the paint.

Pens can be used on unsealed/coated rock (as shown in the sheep rock) however, if the rock is porous the paint will soak into the rock and not show as well.

Paint pens come in two types of paint, oil and water based.

Oil based pens are very durable and are don't usually need more than one coat. These pens also flow well but in some brands, the flow rate can be a little fast.

Water based paint pens work best if you have a very smooth, non porous rock. I find that sometimes I need to go over my designs a second time for better coverage. Many people love Posca brand paint pens.

Sheep and Flowers

To make this simple sheep, look for a round, tan colored stone. Using a white, oil based paint pen, begin to draw the curly circles. Put white dots between the circles.

Draw the head and eyes as shown.
Fill in the eyes with white.
Use gray to color in the head.
Add black circles to the eyes and a make a nose.

Paint the base of the rock with a glossy white acrylic or spray paint.
Draw on the flowers with permanent marker or black paint pen.
Fill in the flowers and leaves.
Add the dots around the flowers, the green vines and vein accents to the leaves.
Draw on the ladybug and color in.

Stone Cacti

The base of the cacti are painted with a medium green acrylic. Add light yellow green streaks to the tops.

For the large cactus, using a white paint pen, draw vertical lines going downward.

Using a dark green paint pen (or acrylic paint with a fine liner brush) make light green marks along the white lines.

With a white paint pen, make small stars along the white lines.

For the medium sized cactus, using an orange paint pen (or acrylic paint if you don't have orange) make a pattern of dots vertically across the width and length.

Using a fine white pen or acrylic paint with liner brush, draw thin lines around the orange dots.

For the Smallest cactus, use the same basic pattern as for the large cactus but make yellow dots in the middle.

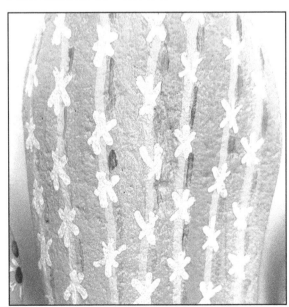

Zentangle

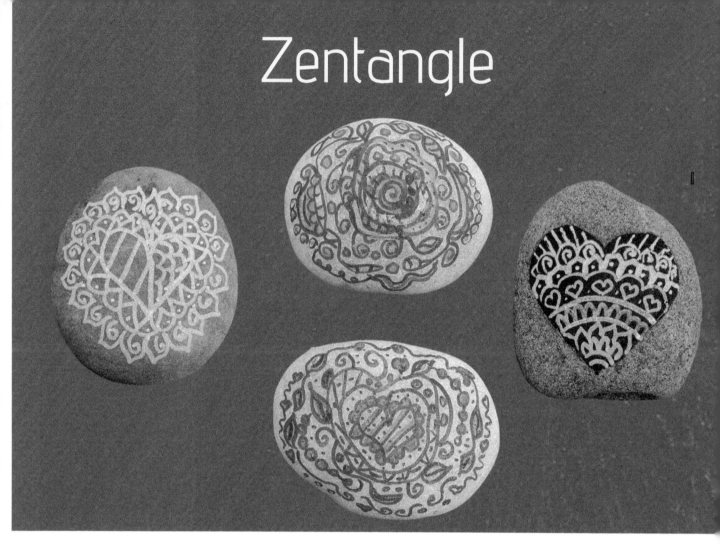

Zentangle is defined as a form of meditative doodling that uses patterns, also called tangles, that flow together to form a zen-tangle.

I discovered zentangle just recently, but really, I've been practicing something very much like it since I was 8 years old. Zentangle is the perfect art form for a non-perfectionist like myself. Hours can go by before I notice the time.

Zentangle needs little in the way of step-by-step instruction, it's something you just need to start doing and then it starts to flow. However, if you need something to get you started, you can find inspiration from a lot of zentangle art online by searching the internet.

Zentangle works great on both natural and painted rock with any kind of writing instrument; markers, highlighters or paint pens.

I love using natural white rocks with highlighter markers for a soft look but it's also fun to use white paint pens on black backgrounds. Experiment with a variety of backgrounds and colors, zentangle is addicting!

The black and white rocks were spray painted black and the pen that was used is called a chalk marker. A chalk marker has good coverage but you can also use any white paint pen.

The heart is a natural colored stone with the white chalk or paint pen.

For the black heart with a natural background (opposite page), you can stencil on a black heart or simply outline a heart with pencil and paint it black. After it is completely dry, using pastel colored, water based paint pens, make a design, starting at the bottom and working upwards.

These stones are naturally white and the highlighter markers give a soft, subtle look to the designs.

It's easiest to start out a zentangle design in the center and work out from that point.

The designs often encircle the center point and move outward.

I like to make the design in one pen color (brown in these stones) and then fill in with color afterwards.

Washi tape is a sticky, masking-like **tape** that is durable and flexible and is available in a variety of widths, textures, patterns and colors.

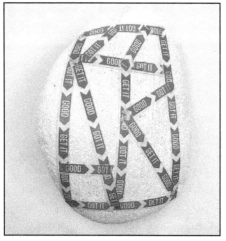

Base coat the rock.

Tape a design on your rock, the tape serves as a barrier and border to the paints.

Paint your desired colors.

After the rock is completely dry, carefully peel off the tape to reveal your design.

You can outline the design with a marker or paint pen for further definition if you like.

Squish Painting

I have named this technique "squish painting" but in truth I have no idea if someone before me has given it a more respectable term. Squish painting is exactly as it's name describes it.

Squish painting is as simple and fun as it gets, and kids love it!.

It works best with thicker acrylic paint (generally sold in tubes).

Base coat your rock.

Place various colors in small amounts around the rock. With this rock I've used some exciting metallic colors: gold, copper and silver.

Place a piece of **wax paper** on the top and gently press down until the colors begin to mingle.

Carefully lift off the wax paper.

This type of painting takes longer to dry than most.

I added the stick on gems but I think it's pretty just the way it is as well.

Marbling

Marbling is one of the most enjoyable and rewarding paint methods for rocks.

To marble you must first get the paint to the right consistency for flowing together so you will need to use a *pouring medium*.

To marble rocks, mix each color of paint separately in a cup with pouring medium. Use the instructions on the bottle of pouring medium to achieve the correct consistency.

Undercoat your rock with acrylic paint.

This is a messy project so make sure you put some wax paper under your project.

Pour a small amount of each color over your rock

After all the colors have been poured, take a tool: dot tool, stylus, pencil or small stick and drag it around the rock, weaving it throughout.

This large, marbled rock is created without the use of a tool.

Base coat a large, smooth rock with white paint.

Mix each color with pouring medium.

Wearing gloves, apply the paint colors in the order shown: Orange, yellow, green, white.

With each new addition of color, tilt and turn the rock with your hands so that the colors run together and swirl.

You can experiement with making your own pouring medium. Mix equal parts of water and white glue in a jar and shake to mix. Add the pouring medium to the paint.
Mix the pouring medium and paint in equal ratios to use on the rocks.

Spray your marbled rocks with sealant when they are dry. The pouring medium makes them feel glossy but it doesn't protect them from the elements.

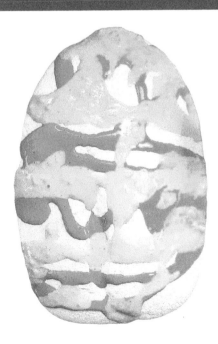

Decoupage

Decoupage is a great way to cover a rock without painting it. You can use napkins, fabric or thin paper.

It takes a bit of practice to position the thin paper or fabric correctly and not to tear it. There's a huge variety of patterns to choose from! In this example I use a thin 2-ply napkin.

Decoupage requires the use of a poly acrylic brush-on varnish.

Brands:
Mod Podge
Decou-page (Americana)
Dura-clear (DecoArt)

Take the napkin and separate the layers.

Coat the base of the rock with a thin layer of varnish.

Place the napkin and then carefully add another layer of varnish on top, being careful not to tear it. Cover the napkin completely.

Let it dry thoroughly, this may take 24 hours.

For the words, use a very thin piece of paper or tissue paper and stamp the saying on it.

Brush some of the varnish on the rock on the area that you want to place your paper.

Carefully place the paper and then brush on more varnish.

TIP:
There's a huge variety of patterns to choose from! For this technique try using fabric, doilies and other thin paper items.

Stickers

Using stickers needs little in the way of instructions. Flat stickers, like these cat a dog stickers, work best on a rock that has a base coat or a thick sealant coat. After you apply the stickers, you can apply another sealant coat so they can be used outside.

There are many different kinds of stickers, these llamas are not flat but rather they are 3 dimensional and they have texture on them.

Although 3-D stickers don't lay flat and therefore cannot be sealed for outside use, they are a super way to decorate some rocks and use in decor or to give as gifts.

TIP:
If you are having trouble getting stickers to adhere to the rocks, simply turn the stickers over onto their backs and spray a very light coat of adhesive onto them before applying.

Polka Dot Rabbit Rock

This project is very simple and it's a great rock to decorate with for Spring.

Paint various colored, pastel dots on the rock.

Let dry and apply stickers. If your stickers are not sticky enough, spray the backs with a light coat of adhesive spray.

You can also spray on a sealant to make this more durable. Test the sealant first to make sure it won't damage the stickers.

A project like this won't hold up well to the elements outside, but it makes a great indoor decoration.

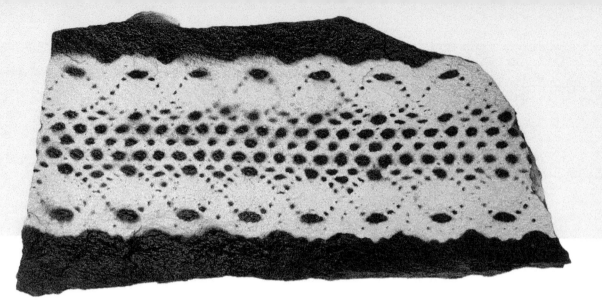

Lace Resists

Lace Resists are a creative way to apply an intricate pattern to a rock without having to painstakingly paint every little detail.

Tips:
Search out old lace at thrift stores or buy new at sewing and craft stores, you don't need much.

You can also use old burlap and other fabrics that have a loose weave.

These pieces are black and white but you can also experiment with colors as well.

You must use spray paint for the top coat, brush on paints will not work.

Also, use a very light touch when spraying, if you spray the paint on too heavily, it will bleed under the lace and ruin the design.

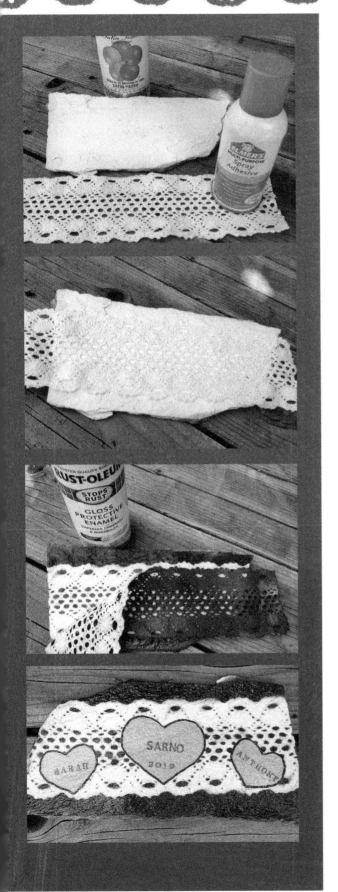

Spray paint a flat, smooth rock with white, let dry.

Lightly spray the back of a piece of lace with spray adhesive.

Place the lace on the rock and press down firmly.

Spray the entire piece with black or another contrasting color. Make sure you spray LIGHTLY. If you spray too much at one time, the paint will bleed under the lace and smear the design.

Peel the lace carefully off the rock to expose the design.

After the paint is dry you can paint a design on top of it either by using a stencil or freehand.

Colorful Cut-out Resist

This project is similar to the lace resists except that, instead of lace, we use cut-outs that are either paper or wood.

To make a colorful resist design, choose a rock that is large enough to accommodate your cut-out.

For this piece I am using a laser-cut wooden wreath. You could also use a paper cut-out.

Using a flat brush, make brush strokes in the colors of your choice. These are the colors that will be showing through. Let it dry throughly.

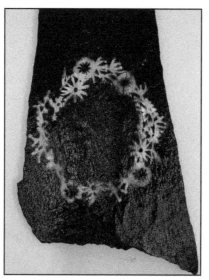

Place the wreath on top of the colors. If it isn't staying put, you can spray a light coat of adhesive on it to help it to stick.

Spray black (or any dark color) paint over the entirety of the pieces. Spray lightly around the wreath.

Lift off the cut-out and the colors will be exposed.

Botanical Resists

There are so many possibilities for botanical resists! In general you will need to use leaves or pressed flowers for this project as it works best when the botanicals you are using are flat. Your rock will need to be flat and somewhat smooth also.

Take a leaf or pressed flower stem and spray it lightly with spray adhesive.

Press the botanical gently to the rock.

Spray very lightly over the botanical and the rock, with spray paint (white or any color of your choosing).

Carefully lift off the botanical.

Spray with a sealant.

That's it! A super easy technique that gives you a fabulous minimalist decor look.

Kids and Rock Painting

There is almost no better art canvas for kids to paint on than rocks. In most areas there is an endless supply of rocks and kids have great imaginations when it comes to painting on them.

Most of the projects in this book are suitable for, or can be adapted to children.

Special tips for Kids and Rocks:

It's important for kids to feel encouraged. Let their imaginations run free. Always praise their efforts, no matter what the artistic outcome.

  * Offer tips in an encouraging way, don't worry about the mess.

  * Make sure you have old clothes and lots of newspapers handy.

  * Help them go online for inspiration if they are lacking ideas.

"Kids love painting on rocks because they know that rock canvases are readily available and there's no pressure to be perfect."

* Paint pens or markers might be less messy and more fun to start learning with.

* Teach them how to do dots and make lines for easy designs.

* Sketch out a design for them, keep it very simple.

* Help them paint their favorite characters.

* Pick very easy projects like pumpkins, rainbows, dots

* Keep the color selection simple so colors don't turn into a muddy look.

* Consider keeping black out of the palette so their colors don't become gray when mixed.

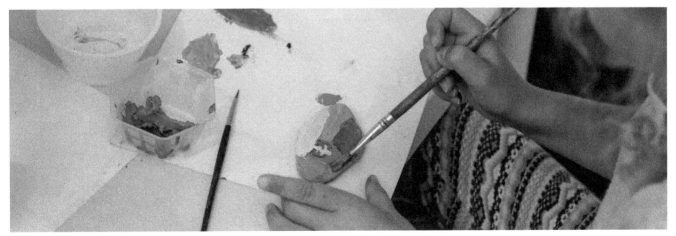

Stone Decor

Stone Art for Decor

Think outside the box when it comes to using stones in decor. You can decorate them with more than paint! The stones pictured are decorated with simple ribbons, dried flowers and moss.

Display your stone art in baskets, near plants and on bookshelves. Stone art can add a touch of the earthy art to any decor.

wood shavings

Moss and dried flowers

Ribbon and dried grasses

Potpourri Rocks

Rocks and potpourri may not seem like a likely combination but they are next to each other in nature all the time.

In the summer I try to walk through my gardens when I'm having coffee in the morning and pick petals to dry for potpourri. One day as I was painting rocks for this book a few petals stuck to a wet rock. At first I was annoyed but then the idea for potpourri rocks flashed into my brain. I love the way they turned out.

For these rocks, spread a thick, white glue onto a natural or painted rock.

Roll the rock in the potpourri petals.

I didn't spray these stones with sealant, I wanted the scent of petals to come through. They are easy to refresh when they get old. Simply scrape of the old petals, add glue and reapply more potpourri.

Pressed Flower Rocks

Flowers and rocks go well together, they contrast strength and delicacy. Who doesn't love a beautiful rock garden? Pressed flowers on rocks are my version of an indoor rock garden.

Pressed flowers work well with rocks because they are flat and easily glued and sealed on. These pressed flower rocks will last a long time.

You can press your own flowers or buy them.

To press your own, simply pick suitable flowers (those without too much thickness are best) and press between an old book (phone books work well) for about two weeks to dry.

To apply flowers to rocks, lightly spray the rocks with spray adhesive and apply your flowers. Your rocks can be painted or natural.

After you apply your flowers by pressing down carefully, spray a light coat of sealant on the top. This preserves the color and keeps the flowers from breaking off.

If your rocks are light enough, you can glue a ribbon to the back to make into a hanging ornament.

Fiber Art Rocks

Rocks wrapped in fiber are a novel way to make some cute, fuzzy rock decor. Needle felting uses woolen batt and a specialized needle to make felted pieces.

Needle felting is a very easy, inexpensive fiber art to get started with. To begin, you will need some wool and a specialized felting needle (see resources below) and a foam pad to work on.

Materials for Poppy scene: Natural colored wool batt, wool top in red, green, yellow, tan, blue. felting needle, foam pad

To make this garden scene, you will first need to make a wool base (to felt onto). Using wool batt, felt the fiber down until it's compact and will hold together. *Felting consists of repeatedly stabbing wool, over and over with a specialized needle, until it matts down and will hold together.*

Draw a circle on the wool base and around the rock to make a guide. Felt on light blue for the sky and a little bit of tan or brown for the earth. Felt down the wool after each addition. Add a bit of yellow for the sun.

To make the stems, twist some green together and felt on by carefully pushing the needle through the stem and into the background.

Add the poppies by making circles of red. Using black, make small circles in the middles, felt down.

Wrap the finished piece around the rock, gluing at the back.

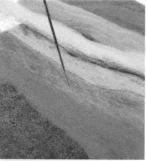

More Felting Tutorials:
www.naturecrafty.com

Wool Resources:
sarafinafiberart.com

Amazon and Etsy - Needle felting supplies

Materials for rainbow rock: wool top (top is a form of processed wool) in blue, purple, green, yellow, orange and red, felting needle, foam pad.

Lay the strips of wool next to each other on the foam pad. Push the needle through the wool to "felt" it together. This will compact the wool and tangle the fibers together so that the strips will become one fabric.

Wrap the fiber around the rock and glue down with hot glue. Go to: www.naturecrafty.com for more detailed needle felting instructions.

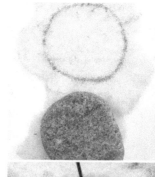

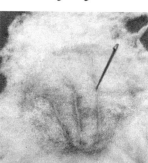

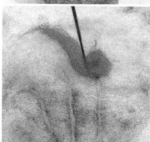

If you want to see traditionally crocheted stones, check out: @moonstone_designs_ on Instagram. Mandy is an expert in crocheting on rocks. When she first started there were no patterns so she adapted doily patterns to fit. She has since developed her own designs for stones and her pieces are beautiful.

To find patterns for crochet for stones, check out ravelry.com.

Crocheted rocks are a fun new way to use your crochet skills. But what if you don't know how to crochet? You can still get this great look in your decor by simply applying some already-crocheted lace.

Choose a piece of crochet that will fit around your rock. Thrift and antique stores are great ways to find bargains on slightly damaged lace and crochet. Old tablecloths and doilies work well too.

Lay the rock on top of the lace and cut around it so that you have enough to wrap around the rock.

Carefully pull the lace around the rock and glue to the back with hot glue. White glue will not work.

Cut a piece of coordinating fabric and glue on top of the back.

That's it! You can make all kinds of pretty, lacy rocks and they look great displayed in bowls or among plants.

Instagram: @moonstone_designs_

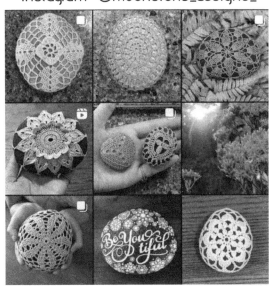

Rock Groups and Communities

Rock painting has become so popular that there are now many groups and online communities centered around this growing trend.

Artists are creating kindness rocks that they paint with happy, uplifting quotes and then hide for strangers to find - and hopefully be encouraged by.

There are thousands of communities participating in the rock painting hide and finds. One group, The Kindness Rocks Project, tries to connect communities by doing seek-and-find rocks with inspirational sayings on them. The group states that, "Our purpose is simple, to cultivate connections within communities and lift others up through simple acts of kindness." Search for them at, www.thekindnessrocksproject.com.

There are hundreds of city specific groups similar to the Kindness Project on Facebook. Simply type in, "Rock groups + your city name" and request to join.

Many online rock painting groups also center around inspirational ideas, tutorials and groups expressly for sharing your work.

Depending on your location, you can possibly find an in-person group to paint with as well. Rock painters are a social group and love to create together.

Clay Rocks

Pressed Clay Rocks

I have made many art objects out of clay in my life but it wasn't until I started writing this book that I thought of covering rocks with polymer clay. This is the technique that gave me a lot of joy this summer. I loved walking through the garden and picking flowers to make into these pieces.

Polymer clay is flexible clay that bakes hard in the home oven. It goes under the brand names of Sculpy, Fimo and Cernit among others.

1. Choose a smooth stone for this project. Pick flowers and grasses that are a bit on the flat side as they press into the clay better.

2. Roll out your clay with a rolling pin. It should be about 1/4" thick. Any thinner or thicker and the clay will tend to crack after it hardens. Place the clay carefully around the top and as you pull it around to the back you can choose to cover the rock completely or just the front and sides.

3. Press the flowers into the clay and if needed and give a little roll with the rolling pin. Do not press the rolling pin into with too much force, use a light touch. Remove the flowers with tweezers if needed.

4. Cover a pan with foil or parchment to protect the baking sheet. Making sure your stone is at room temperature before baking and bake according to package directions. It is extremely important to follow manufactures directions as this clay can burn easily.

5. After the clay is cool, you can paint your flowers. Mix acrylic paints with small amounts of water for the soft, water color look. Actual water colors do not work on the polymer stones. Lightly paint on your colors.

These are for indoor use.

Seasonal
Rock Art
Projects

Christmas rocks

Christmas is the perfect time to paint rocks! Kids love giving them as gifts. If the rocks aren't too heavy, you can glue ribbons on the back of them to hang on the tree.

Make a new Christmas tradition to paint rocks together for gift giving and decorating.

TIP:
Stock up on metallic paints as they look great for Christmas painting.

Paint the base coat with a metallic gold.

Add the snowman, his buttons, eyes, nose, hat and scarf. I used paint pens but you can also use paint.

Paint the banner and let dry.

Add the snowflakes with a dot tool.

Outline the design with a fine tip, permanent marker. Add "Let it snow" onto the banner.
Add the arms with fine tip marker.

Christmas stencils are available in almost every craft store. Choose a small set to use on rocks.

Paint the background of the rock in your chosen color.

Stencil with a sponge.

To add snow, put a small amount of paint on the end of a dry, wide brush or toothbrush.

Flick the brush with your fingers to splatter paint onto the rock.

Zentangle is great for making Christmas shapes.

Paint the rock with a metallic green, let dry.

Start by very lightly sketching a triangle with a pencil.

Fill inside the triangle with white paint pen in a zentangle design and then add a red star and red berries.

This JOY rock is essentially a dot rock.

Paint the background with metallic silver.

After it's dry, draw on the letters with permanent marker.

Begin filling in with various sizes and colors of dots.

For the larger dots, add layers of dots within them.

Paint the inside of the letters with white.

Spray with a sealant that's safe for markers.

Paint a rock with a white base coat.

Write "Merry Christmas" in cursive with a fine tip, permanent marker. Look up cursive fonts online and practice first if you feel you need to.

To paint the pine cones and greens start with a dark brown. The pine comes are simple coma strokes.

Add the greens and the berries. The greens are made with a fine liner brush and thin strokes.

Spring Rocks

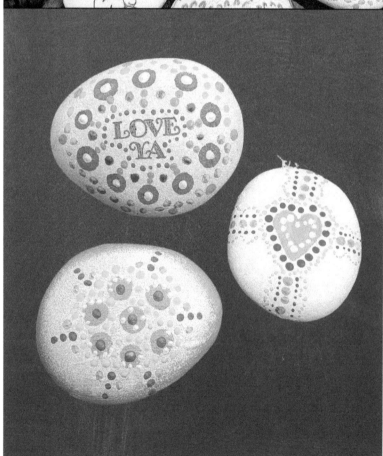

Painting Spring and Easter rocks are as much fun as dying Easter eggs. I collect egg shaped rocks throughout the year to use in the Spring.

You can even substitute painted rocks for eggs at egg hunts. It's fun to put names on them and sayings that children will enjoy.

Painted Spring rocks are a great and inexpensive way to decorate for the holidays.

Dot painting and mandalas in spring colors are pretty. .

You can make a variety of designs with the same pastel colors to give a coordinated look.

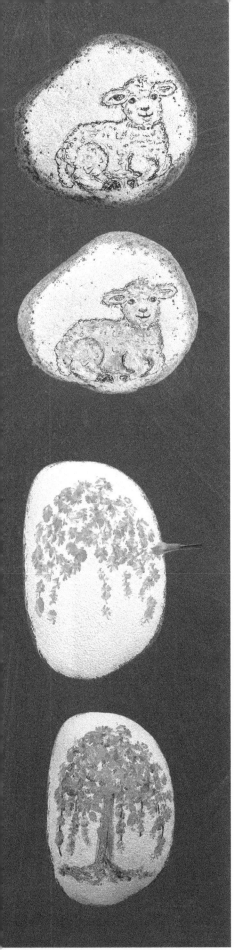

Sheep

To make this simple sheep start by sponging on a white background.

Trace a sheep onto the background with a permanent fine tip marker.

Use the watercolor acrylic method to fill in the sheep with soft color.

Tree

To paint this Weeping Cherry tree, Sponge on a white background and BEFORE the background is dry use a brush dipped in pink paint to dab on the blossoms.
You won't be making strokes, just dabbing the brush.

The white and pink paint will mix to make petals that look realistic.

After the petals and background are dry, paint in the trunk with brown and add a few green leaves.

Add light green grass to the bottom.

Egg

Easter eggs are easy to make with ric-rac trim.

Wrap the ric-rac around the egg, secure with a tiny bit of hot glue to hold it fast.

Paint around the ric-rac.

Lift of the ric-rac to expose the design.

Outline the edges with puffy paint.

Summer Rocks

Flag

To make this flag rock, spray paint the base of the rock with a glossy black spray paint.

The flag itself is drawn on with paint pens.
Make an outline and draw the stripes and hearts with white paint pen.

Fill in the flag with red, blue and white.

Spray with a sealant.

Fish

To make a fish like this you will need a smooth, oblong stone.

Paint the stone a base coat of medium blue.

Draw on the face, gills and fins.

Using a dry brush, take white and light yellow paint, mix on the brush and wipe the brush on a piece of paper, then lightly paint in strokes around the drawn in lines. Add a dot of white to the eye and edges of the fins.

Fireworks

Fireworks rocks are exciting for kids.

There are two ways to make fireworks.

1. Use a glitter glue to draw on the fireworks.

2. Using a white puffy paint, draw on the fireworks and then sprinkle your chosen glitter into it before it dries.

Seaglass

These are not technically rocks but actually sea glass. You can find them where you find rocks and they are so pretty when painted I decided to include them in this section.

To make painted seaglass, use a paint pen or white marker to draw small, zentangle designs. They look great displayed in sand in a bowl.

Crabby at the Beach

On this page I show you why it's so fun to add a non-painted item to your rocks. Buy paper items like this crab in the sticker section of your local craft store.

These are best as indoor rocks

To make the crabby rock, first paint your rock a base coat of white.

Using a thick, white glue, make a layer of glue at the base of the rock.

Add the sand and bits or rock and shells and press into the glue.

Glue the Crab on. Crabs like this are availbe in the sticker section of craft stores.

Finally, you can stamp a saying, date or place on the rock.

This seagull is needle felted. You can find instructions for him at www.naturecrafty.com

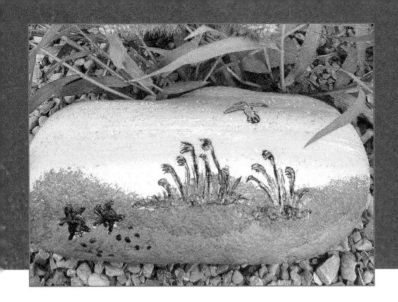

Seaside Scene

When we went on vacation to the beach, the kids and I would always paint some rocks to remind us of the seaside.

Paint the rock with a white base coat.

Load blue and white onto a flat (side) brush and paint the background of the sky.

To make the sand, put two dots of tan and brown next to each other, pick up the paint with a sponge and swirl it slightly.
Dab the sponge across the width of the rock with a light touch to make sand.

The baby turtles are dark brown.

Paint the seagrass. I used two colors, light and dark green.

Paint the seagull with white, gray and black.

Spray with a sealant.

Autumn Rocks

Owl

Dry brushing for feathers is an easy technique. Simply put paint onto a dry brush then stroke the paint brush onto a piece of paper until the strokes look like the above picture.

I love owls and owls are popular birds in the world of crafting. My aunt gave me a rock owl as a child and I still keep it as a treasure. You never know how your hand painted rock might be cherished by someone someday.

Paint a round rock white. This rock happens not to be super smooth but I liked the texture.

Paint black eyes and a beak.

Using the dry brush method, brush on some reddish brown feathers.

Add yellow around the face and as highlights on the wings.

Dry brush some tan on the chest.

Add brown to the iris of the eyes and white reflection spots.

With a matching brown marker, go around the feathers on the wing and the neck.

This fall leaf rock looks great with a light, natural rock background. You can spray sealant on the rock first (so you can erase mistakes more easily) or you can leave it au natural.

Put a leaf stencil down on the rock.

Use two colors of paint on a sponge, I've used a burnt orange and a mustard yellow.

Dab the sponge on some paper to mix the colors and to reduce the amount of paint on the sponge.

Gently dab the sponge into the leaf stencils.

Draw on acorns with a brown marker.

Write your chosen phrase.

Fall Leaves

Everyone loves the mascot of fall - pumpkins! This pumpkin is a bit of a twist as it's not a round rock but a flat one.

Pumpkins can be made with all sorts of shapes and sizes.

To make this pumpkin, I glued a tiny pebble stem onto the top.

Pumpkins look great if you can create streaks of colors as vertical lines.

Mix orange and yellow together on a flat brush and apply long strokes. The colors will mingle as you are brushing on the paint.

Flat Pumpkin

Rocks

In the search bar of your browser, type"rocks" and then the name of the following websites to pull up the best sellers.

Amazon

Etsy

Michaels

HobbyLobby

Paints

Paints can be purchased online and in craft stores. The brands we used:

Americana

Martha Stewart

Folk Art

DecoArt

Ceramcoat

Most of these supplies can be found in big box craft stores but if you want to buy online, simply type the name of the brand into the search bar plus what the item is. For example: "Martha Stewart Paints". This will bring up a large variety of companies you can buy from.

Paint Pens

Brands used for rock painting:

Sharpie oil based

Posca oil based

Artistro

Markers

Sharpie Permanent markers

Sakura Gelly Roll

Signo Uniball

Stencils

Martha Stewart brand

Folk Art

The Stencil Company

Dot tools

The Happy Dotting Company

Amazon

Micheals

Simple, fun crafts with wool! On Amazon!

More Books by Lori Rea

Needle Felting
A Complete Course

From Beginner to Advanced
with Step-by-Step Instructions

Lori Rea

Needle Felting
For Beginners

Easy Projects   Basic Techniques   Supplies

Lori Allen Rea

Ingram Content Group UK Ltd.
Milton Keynes UK
UKHW050030250523
422284UK00003B/42